My Adoption Journey

Journey

The Story Of My Adoption

These are my personal thoughts,
memories, feelings and experiences.

HOLT INTERNATIONAL

Uplifting children. Strengthening families.

For all adoptees around the world –
your stories deserve to be honored.

My Adoption Journey

By: _____

My Self Portrait

What does it mean to be adopted?

I think it means:

_____

_____

_____

_____

_____

_____

_____

What Adoption Means

My Feelings About My Adoption

Meeting your new family can be exciting and scary all at the same time. These are some feelings you might have about meeting your new family and being adopted: happy, sad, scared, excited, curious, angry, nervous, or worried. It's okay to feel all of these things and more. Your new family is feeling all of these things too.

Circle the different feelings you have about your adoption:

Nervous

Happy

Curious

Sad

Scared

Angry

Excited

Confused

Worried

What are some other feelings you have about your adoption?

_____

_____

_____

_____

My Feelings About Adoption

Things That Make Me Feel

Happy

 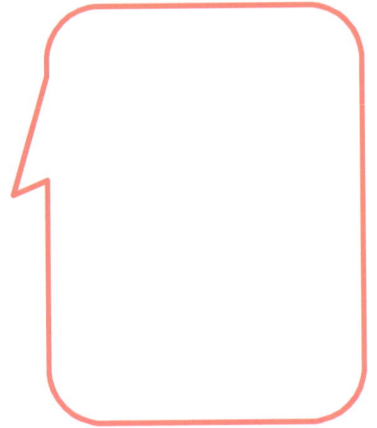

Angry

Brave

Worried

Excited

Bored

Safe

Afraid

Proud

Ashamed

Special

Big Feelings

Sometimes our feelings can feel really big and overwhelming. If your big feelings were like an ocean wave, what would they look like? How tall would the wave be? Would the wave be one color or a whole bunch of colors mixed together? Color the wave with your big and overwhelming feelings.

Calming Strategies

When we encounter large waves of emotions, we can use relaxing strategies to help calm the wave. Each person has different calming preferences. It is helpful to try many different activities to see which strategy works best for you! Use the spaces below to write in your own strategies.

Listen to music (quiet/loud, calming/upbeat)	Swing on an outside swing or hammock
Jump: with a jump rope, on a trampoline, do jumping jacks	Suck on a piece of hard candy (like a Lemonhead)
Hang upside down: lie on the couch with your head on the floor or bend over and touch your toes for 30 seconds	Do Yoga for 10 minutes – have set poses you do and always include downward dog
Take a walk	Run in place or around the yard
Do a chair push/pull or wall pushups	Blow bubbles
Chew on something (gum, chewable jewelry, a toy designated for chewing)	7-11 Breath or breathe like a bear: 7 seconds inhale, 11 seconds exhale
Squeeze a toy like a stress ball or squishy stuffed animal	Have a pillow fight with your stuffed animals
Smell something with the scent of: lavender, lemon or jasmine	Kick a soccer ball into a goal or dribble a ball and shoot baskets
Play with a glitter jar	Rock in a rocking chair

In the water, in the leaves of the palm tree, or on the umbrella, write the calming strategies you use to help the giant waves become smooth waters.

My Favorite Things

When your forever family learned they would be able to adopt you, they wanted to learn everything they could about you! They wanted to know your favorite color, food, activity, sport, subject in school, what you want to do when you grow up, and on and on! What would you like your forever family to know about you?

Tell your forever family about yourself:

_____

_____

_____

_____

_____

_____

Me and My
Favorite Things

These are some more of my favorite things

Games:_____

Toys:_____

Treats:_____

Friends:_____

Activities:_____

Songs:_____

Colors:_____

Sounds:_____

Things to do with family and friends:

_____

_____

Food:_____

Recipe for my favorite food:

_____

_____

_____

_____

_____

_____

_____

_____

_____

Let's Explore!

You live in a big and beautiful country with so much to see and do. When your adoptive family comes to meet you, they want to learn all about your life. Are there places you want to take them? Things you want to show them? Food you want them to try? People you want them to meet? Write it down so you can show them the list when they come.

1. _____

2. _____

3. _____

4. _____

5. _____

6. _____

7. _____

8. _____

9. _____

10._____

11._____

12._____

13._____

14._____

15._____

What is Safety?

Your adoptive parents will do everything they can to help you feel safe and secure both physically and emotionally.

Parents keep children **physically safe** by creating boundaries and guidelines for video game and internet use, providing structure, food and clothing along with a stable home and place for you to sleep.

Parents keep children **emotionally safe** by having healthy boundaries, listening to you, encouraging you to tell them what you want and need, treating you with kindness and respect, celebrating your accomplishments, offering you comfort when you are sad, and modeling and teaching you how to express yourself.

What do you imagine might help you feel safe and secure with your new adoptive family?

_____

_____

_____

What could your adoptive parents do to help gain your trust?

_____

_____

_____

Bandage Activity

One easy and fun way to build trust with your family members, while practicing how to give care and receive care from them, is by playing the BANDAGE Activity. You can play with your parents, siblings, and friends; you just need a partner and a few Bandages (or Bandage stickers).

If you're playing with a group, pair up with the person next to you. Decide who will be Partner ONE and Partner TWO.

Partner ONE asks Partner TWO, "May I please put a bandage on you?" Wait for Partner TWO's response. It is always okay to say "no" as long as the participant uses respectful words.

If they say, "yes." Partner ONE asks, "Do you have a hurt on the inside or outside?" Wait for response from Partner TWO.

Ask partner TWO to point to which bandage they would like to choose.

Partner ONE puts a bandage on partner TWO's hurt while making eye contact and saying, "I'm so sorry you're hurt." Partner ONE asks partner TWO if he/she would like to tell you about their hurt.

Repeat activity with the roles swapped.

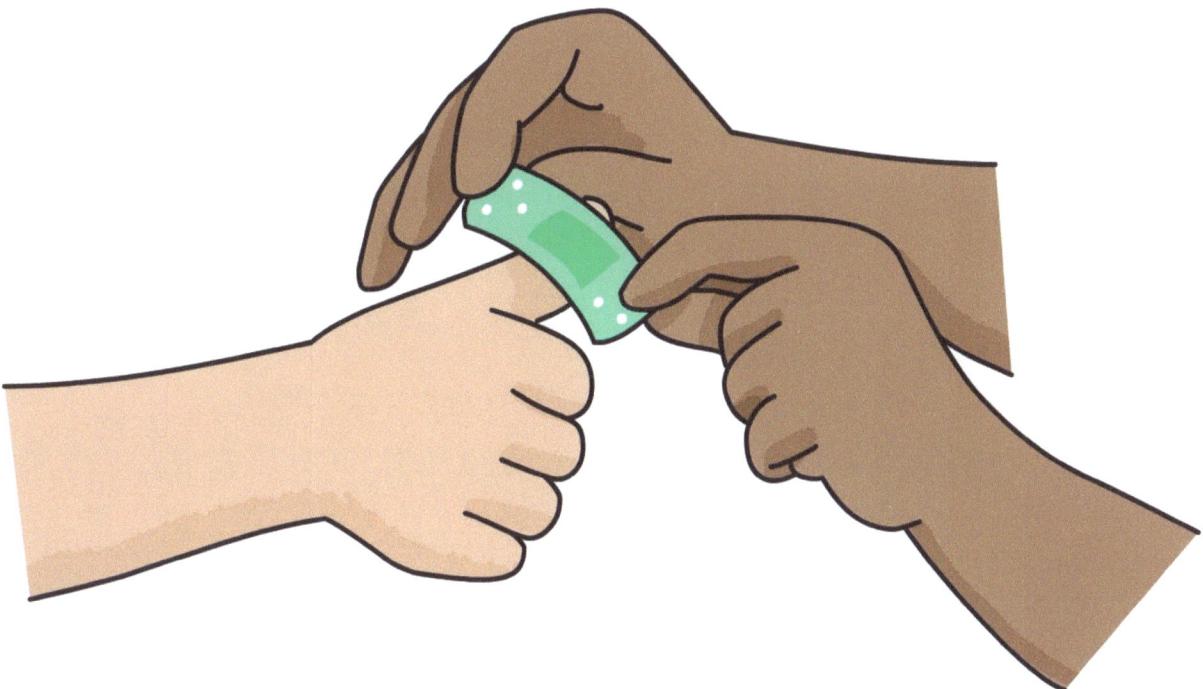

Healthy Ways to Give and Receive Love

Parents show their love in many ways. These are just some of the ways your forever family can show you that they love and care about you. Color a red heart beside all the ways you are comfortable receiving love from your adoptive parents. Write down any other ways you want them to show their love.

High Fives   Giving Smiles

Thumbs Up   Tokens of Appreciation

Blowing Kisses   Brushing My Hair

Wrestling or Rough-Housing   Giving Hugs

Holding Hands   Helping Me with Homework

Teaching Me New Things   Cooking My Favorite Foods

Playing Games   Comforting Me When I Am Sad

Tucking Me in Bed at Night

Giving Me Encouragement   Giving Pats on The Back

Playing Outside with Me   Giving Me Compliments

Saying I Love You

Can you think of other ways you want to receive love from your parents?

_____

_____

_____

_____

Just like there are many ways for your adoptive parents to show you their love, there are many ways you can show your adoptive family that you love and care about them. What are some ways you want to show love and affection to your adoptive family?

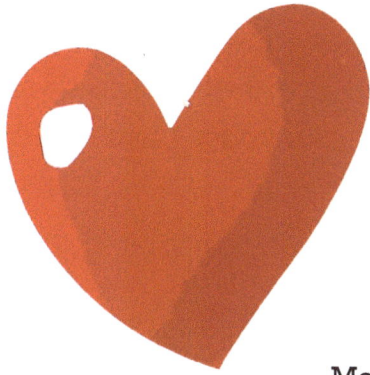

Sharing My Memories

Giving Thumbs Up   Giving Them Hugs

Offering to Help Around the House

Using Kind and Respectful Words and Actions

Making Things for Them   Telling Them How I Feel

Trying New Activities With Them

Playing Games With Them

Blowing Them Kisses   Giving High Fives

Holding Their Hand

Saying I Love You

Can you think of other ways you could show love and affection to your adoptive family?

_____

_____

_____

_____

Love is More Than Hugs and Kisses

Being loved doesn't mean that your parents will buy you everything you want and will say YES to everything you want to do. Having rules, consequences and saying NO are important parts of being a loving parent. These are some more ways that parents show their children they love them. Parents show love when they: listen to their children, care that their children feel sad, have rules to teach their children positive behavior, tell them they did a good job, encourage them to do their best, worry about them. Can you think of other ways parents can show their children they love them?

The most important qualities of a good mom are:

_____

_____

The most important qualities of a good dad are:

_____

_____

If I were a parent, these are some things I would want to do with my children:

_____

_____

Some things I would want to do for them are:

_____

_____

If I were a parent, some things I would never do are:

_____

_____

The most important thing to me about my new family is:

_____

_____

Important People in My Life

There are many important people in everyone's lives. Different people can be important to you for many different reasons. Important people can include parents, other family members, foster families, caregivers, teachers, social workers, friends and more! Make a list of the people that are important to you.

My _____ named _____ is important to me because

_____

_____

My _____ named _____ is important to me because

_____

_____

My _____ named _____ is important to me because

_____

_____

My _____ named _____ is important to me because

_____

_____

My _____ named _____ is important to me because

_____

_____

My _____ named _____ is important to me because

_____

_____

These are the people who are special to me. I carry them in my heart.

My Caregivers

You have had many people in your life who have taken care of you. Birth family are those people to whom you are biologically related, but are not always the people that take care of you. Your caregivers could have been birth family or other people you consider your family, or caregivers from the group care or orphanage you lived in. Think about those people who have cared for you and list them below.

My caregivers have included:

_____

_____

My favorite caregiver is:_____

Other people I lived with:

_____

_____

Some things I liked about my caregivers:

_____

_____

Some things I didn't like about my caregivers:

_____

_____

The places I lived:

_____

_____

Some things nearby:

_____

_____

Things I miss about living here:

_____

_____

_____

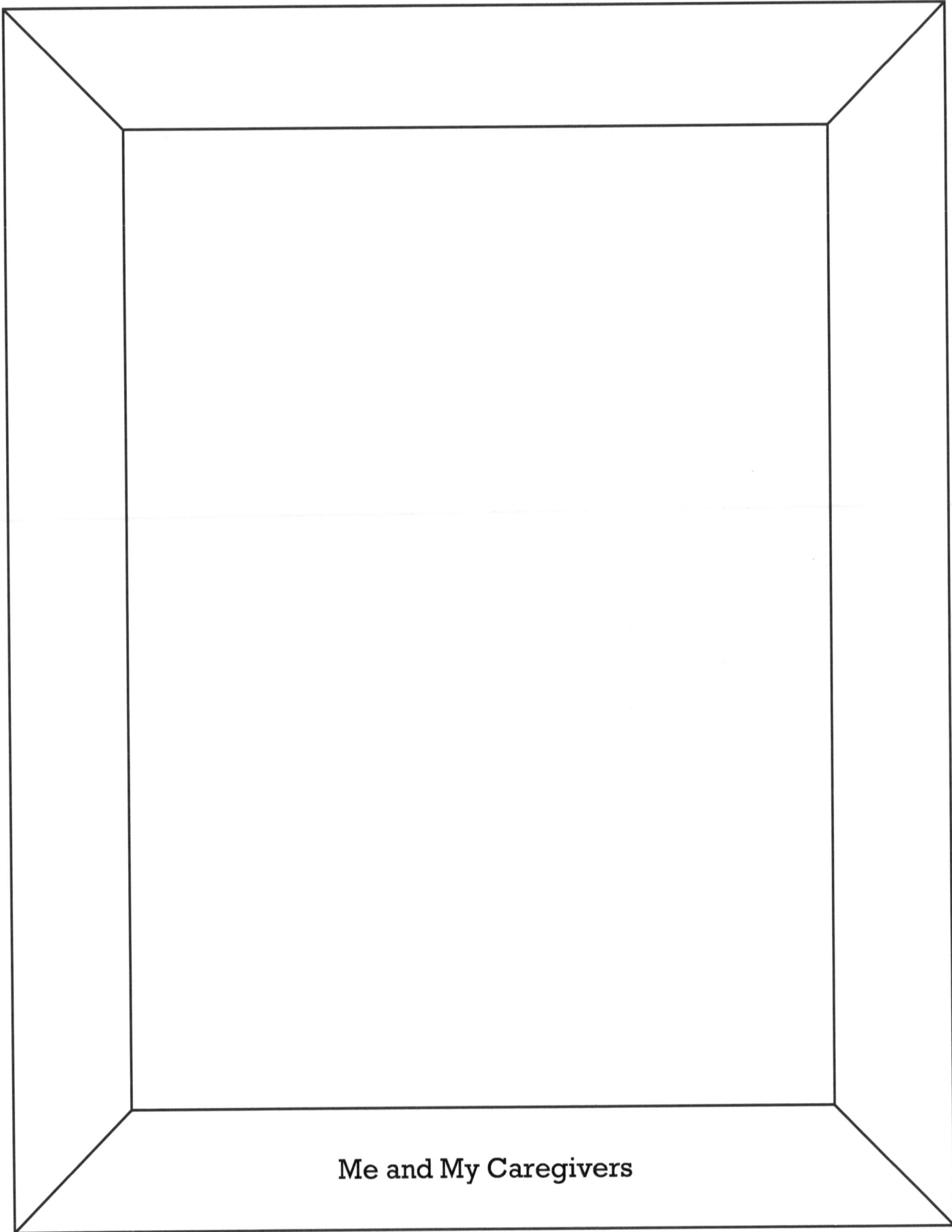

Me and My Caregivers

Places I Have Lived

Special Memories

Have you ever been on a trip or an outing?
Where did you go? What did you like about it?

_____

_____

_____

What are your favorite holidays? What do you do to celebrate them?

_____

_____

_____

What makes you laugh?

_____

_____

_____

What do you enjoy doing? Why do you enjoy doing it?

_____

_____

_____

What do you like best about yourself?

_____

_____

_____

If you had three wishes, what would they be?

_____

_____

_____

School Memories

I am in the _____ grade in school

Special Friends

Things I like to do in school:

My favorite school subject is:

My teacher is:

What my teachers say about me:

Special memories about school:

My Thoughts and Feelings

You might have a lot of different feelings about adoption. Sometimes it helps to write our thoughts and feelings down. If you want to draw your thoughts and feelings instead, use the space on the next page to draw your thoughts and feelings about adoption.

Sometimes I think about:

_____

_____

_____

_____

_____

_____

_____

_____

_____

_____

_____

_____

_____

_____

_____

_____

_____

_____

_____

_____

_____

_____

_____

My Thoughts and Feelings About Adoption

Thoughts from Others

You have many people who care about you including your caregivers, friends, teachers, and more. These pages are for those people to write down their thoughts and memories about you and their wishes for you in the future.

_____

_____

_____

_____

_____

_____

_____

_____

_____

_____

_____

_____

_____

_____

_____

_____

_____

_____

_____

_____

_____

More Thoughts from Others